DASH Diet For Beginners

40 Delicious Recipes And 8 Weeks Of Diet Plans

By Martin Rowland

The trademarks that are used are without any consent, and the publication of the trademark is without permission or backing by the trademark owner. All trademarks and brands within this book are for clarifying purposes only and are the owned by the owners themselves, not affiliated with this document.

Disclaimer – Please read!

The information provided in this book is designed to provide helpful information on the subjects discussed. This book is not meant to be used, nor should it be used, to diagnose or treat any medical condition. For diagnosis or treatment of any medical problem, consult your own physician. The publisher and author are not responsible for any specific health or allergy needs that may require medical supervision and are not liable for any damages or negative consequences from any treatment, action, application or preparation, to any person reading or following the information in this book. References are provided for informational purposes only and do not constitute endorsement of any websites or other sources. Readers should be aware that the websites listed in this book may change.

Table of Contents

Chapter One: What is the DASH Diet?

A history of the DASH Diet

In 2010, the National Heart, Lung, and Blood Institute (NHLBI) sponsored two studies, titled DASH and DASH-Sodium. DASH stands for Dietary Approaches to Stop Hypertension, and the idea behind the studies was simple: find out if changes in diet can lead to a reduction in blood pressure.

The studies were conducted by dividing participants into three groups. For the DASH study, members of one group ate a standard North American diet, another was placed on a similar diet with more vegetables and fruit, and one group was placed on the DASH diet. The results were fantastic. Participants in the DASH group showed a significant lowering of blood pressure and an improvement in overall health.

The DASH-Sodium diet was conducted in a similar fashion. All of the groups were placed on the DASH diet, but the levels of sodium they ate varied. One group consumed the standard amount of sodium for most people, 3,300mg per day. Another consumed 2,300mg per day, and the last group had 1,500mg per day. The difference between the groups was pronounced; they all experienced an improvement in blood pressure, but the improvement was greater for those who had consumed the least salt.

Obviously, these studies were great news for the NHLBI. The diet has become big news since then, winning awards from the US News and World Report five years in a row.

Understanding High Blood Pressure

A lot of people are familiar with high blood pressure, but don't really know what it means. Since we're going to be talking about it a lot, let's go over the basics.

According to the American Heart Association (AHA), blood pressure is measured in two ways: systolic and diastolic. A typical blood pressure measurement looks like this: 117/76 mm Hg. The top number is the systolic blood pressure reading; it is always the higher number of the two, and it represents the amount of pressure that is in the arteries when your heart is beating. The bottom number is the diastolic reading; this represents the amount of pressure in the arteries between heartbeats.

Generally speaking, your systolic blood pressure should be below 120 and your diastolic number should be below 80. If the systolic number is between 120 and 139, that means you are in prehypertension: your blood pressure is too high, but it hasn't yet crossed the line into hypertension. A systolic number over 140 means you have crossed that threshold. Don't panic, though: it is possible to have a systolic reading of 140 or over once without actually having high blood pressure. If your doctor is worried about you after one high reading, they will take a few more and build up a clear picture. If the reading remains consistently over 140, it's time to make some changes.

The "mm Hg" part means "millimeters of mercury". This is actually a unit of pressure, one so tiny that it isn't used for much beyond measuring how much pressure is being put on arteries (although it's used for some other medical purposes, like measuring cerebrospinal fluid pressure). The "points" that people refer to when it comes to blood pressure typically refer to the systolic reading. This number will start going down when you begin the DASH diet.

Health Benefits

According to the Mayo Clinic, the DASH diet can reduce systolic blood pressure by between seven and twelve points when used consistently over a long period. However, it is possible to see a drop of a few points in just a couple of weeks.

There were also reductions in cholesterol levels among study participants; this makes sense, as the diet is naturally designed to be heart-healthy and low in unnecessary fats.

Since the initial studies, it has become clear that the DASH diet is good for more than just blood pressure; it also has benefits for people looking to lose weight, and is a boon for diabetics. While weight loss isn't the aim of the DASH diet, it is a fairly reliable side effect of eating an overall healthier diet and reducing your fat and salt intake.

After a few weeks on the DASH diet you will notice an increase in energy, an improvement in your overall health, and possibly some weight loss (particularly if you exercise). It's possible to tailor your diet and exercise program to your lifestyle in order to get the most out of it; we'll cover that in more detail later on.

The Diet Itself

The DASH diet isn't a fad, so don't worry: no one's expecting you to live on smoothies and kale. It mainly consists of low-fat dairy products, fruit and vegetables, lean meats and poultry, grains (ideally whole), nuts, seeds, beans, and fish. You can also have fats and oils, but in moderation. So, for example, if your typical meal is a steak with some potatoes, it could now become chicken with some green vegetables and brown rice. This may seem like a huge change, but it's surprisingly easy to get used to. There are also plenty of lean red meats, so you don't have to sacrifice steak altogether! Another example is something simple: how you take your coffee. Before, you might have had a strong cup of joe with cream and sugar. On the DASH diet, you can switch to decaf (depending on what your doctor says), with artificial sweetener and skim milk. If you drink a few cups of coffee a day, you've just found one small way to make a big difference.

Before you start planning menus, it's important to know what the food you will be eating is going to do for you. This table is made up of information from the NHLBI, and it will give you an idea of exactly what each food group can do for you and why they are so important.

DASH Diet Food Groups

Food Group: Lean meats, fish, and poultry
Examples: Any lean meat or any cuts you can remove fat from. Think chicken, pork, loin beef cuts, lamb, and turkey. Look out for the word "loin", this means it will be lean.
How it fits into the DASH diet: These meats are full of magnesium and protein, which are essential sources of energy. Protein gives you an energy boost with very little fat; that's why bodybuilders are so fond of it. Magnesium helps your body to process food and can reduce blood pressure.

Food Group: Low-fat and fat free dairy products
Examples: Skim milk, low-fat cheeses, low-fat yogurt, and any fat-free dairy product.
How it fits into the DASH diet: Dairy is a vital source of calcium, and you can still get what you need for healthy bones and teeth from low-fat options. Dairy is another great source of protein, too.

Food Group: Vegetables
Examples: Look out for green, leafy vegetables. Green beans, broccoli, potatoes, yams, and tomatoes are all good. Collard greens, squash, and lima beans are great too.
How it fits into the DASH diet: Vegetables are full of fiber, which you need to stay healthy and avoid bloating. They are also a source of potassium, which is great for your heart, and magnesium.

Food Group: Fruit
Examples: Most fruits are good, so pick your favorites.

How it fits into the DASH diet: Like vegetables, fruit is full of magnesium, fiber, and potassium. It's also a good way to relieve any cravings you have for something sweet.

Food Group: Grains
Examples: Anything whole wheat or whole grain is a good alternative to white bread products. Look for whole wheat pasta, brown rice, pita bread, and bagels for meals. For snacks, unsalted pretzels and popcorn are better than chips or cookies.
How it fits into the DASH diet: Whole grains are bursting with fiber and energy. If you eat the right grains instead of white bread or pasta, you will find yourself feeling fuller for longer. Grains also give you a sustained energy boost, reducing any cravings for coffee and sweets.

Food Group: Nuts, legumes, and seeds
Examples: Most seeds are good, but be careful: some nuts are very fatty, especially the roasted and salted varieties. Look out for peanuts, sunflower seeds, hazelnuts, and almonds. When it comes to mealtimes, add kidney beans, split peas, or lentils to soups and stews.
How it fits into the DASH diet: These are full of protein and energy. Nuts, seeds, and legumes are also a great source of fiber and magnesium, and they make for very healthy snacks.

Food Group: Fats and oils
Examples: Margarine, canola, corn, or olive oil, light mayonnaise and low-fat salad dressing are all good choices.
How it fits into the DASH diet: These aren't ideal, but they won't hurt in small doses. It will certainly help you to add some extra flavor to salads and other foods you may not be used to.

Food Group: Sweets and added sugar
Examples: Avoid these as much as you can, but when you do eat sweets go for ones made with natural flavors, rather than added sugars. Try hard candies and gelatin with fruit flavorings, or maple candy. For colder treats, look out for sorbet instead of ice cream.

How it fits into the DASH diet: Sugar isn't a recommended part of the DASH diet, but you can treat yourself now and then.

The DASH-Sodium diet is pretty much the same as the DASH diet, but the amount of sodium you can have is reduced from 2,300mg per day to 1,500mg. Some people are advised to start with the DASH-Sodium diet for optimal results. According to the NHLBI, if you already have high blood pressure (typically defined as a systolic reading of 140 or higher), have a chronic kidney condition, are 51 or older, or are African-American, you should start out with the reduced sodium intake. The studies found that people who already had high blood pressure showed the most improvement at the beginning of the DASH-Sodium diet.

Typically, the diet will allow you to have a certain amount of servings from each food group every day. Consuming anything outside the diet, such as alcoholic beverages, is best kept to a minimum; if your doctor says you can treat yourself, go ahead, but don't go overboard. As long as the servings are regulated and you stick to the portions, you will notice a difference.

Chapter Two: Implementing the DASH Diet

Understanding the Diet

The first thing to do is figure out the diet that works for you. Depending on your needs, that may be DASH or DASH-Sodium. Once you've worked that out, you can start looking at your calorie intake. The amount of calories you need per day depends on how much exercise you do, and how active you are in general.

According to the NHLBI, there are three activity levels: sedentary, moderately active, and active. People with sedentary lifestyles don't undertake much physical activity: even with an extra 30 minutes of activity per day, you would be considered sedentary if you don't do much beyond, say, walking from your car to work, occasionally walking the dog, and a bit of housework. Moderately active people, according to the NHLBI, undertake activity on a daily basis that is the calorie-burning equivalent of walking 1.5-3 miles per day, at around 3-4 miles per hour, in addition to standard activities like housework etc. Moderately active people may cycle to work instead of driving, take their dog on long walks, or take some kind of exercise a couple of times a week (such as running or swimming). Active people are the ones who undertake a little more activity – the equivalent of walking more than three miles a day at 3-4 miles per hour. This could involve daily exercise plus cycling to work and participation in sports on a regular basis.

Think about your lifestyle, and don't forget to take your job into account if you have one. A busy nurse, for example, will be more active on a daily basis than a programmer who spends their day at a desk. If in doubt, choose the lowest activity level to start with and work your way up after a week or two. Consulting with your doctor is a good idea at this point: they can give you a realistic idea of your fitness and activity level if you're unsure.

Calorie-counting doesn't sound like fun, but it's important, particularly at the beginning when you are getting used to a new way of eating and living. This chart, consisting of data from the NHLBI, should give you a good idea of how many calories you should take in per day.

Calorie Requirement Based on Activity Level

Gender	Age	Sedentary	Moderately Active	Active
Female	19-30	2,000	2,000-2,200	2,400
	31-50	1,800	2,000	2,200
	51+	1,600	1,800	2,000-2,200
Male	19-30	2,400	2,600-2,800	3,000
	31-50	2,200	2,400-2,600	2,800-3,000
	51+	2,000	2,200-2,400	2,400-2,800

So, you've worked out how many calories you're allowed per day and promptly panicked when you read the calorie count for some of your favorite foods. Don't worry, that's a normal part of dieting! Now it's time to look at portions.

The DASH diet centers on eating the right foods, but it's crucial that you eat them in the right amounts. If you eat too much dairy and not enough protein, for example, you'll miss out on crucial nutrients that are necessary to get you through the day. It will also reduce the positive impact of the diet if your portions are off, because it is worked out specifically to ensure you get the right amount of good fats (unsaturated fats) and a low amount of bad fats (saturated fats).

The chart below uses information from the NHLBI, and it's a great tool for working out how much you should be eating at any given time. Look at how many calories you should be eating per day to calculate how many servings to have. Serving sizes that are not listed here are easy to work out; many foods list them on the packaging.

Food Group	Servings per Day (according to calorie allowance)			Serving Sizes
	1,600	**2,000**	**2,600**	
Meats and fish	3-6	6 or less	6	1 ounce, or 1 egg
Dairy	2-3	2-3	3	1 cup of yogurt or milk, or 1½ ounces of cheese
Vegetables	3-4	4-5	5-6	1 cup of raw, leafy vegetables, 1½ cups of raw or cooked vegetables, cut up, or 1½ cups of vegetable juice
Fruit	4	4-5	5-6	1 medium fruit, ¼ cup of dried fruit, 1½ cups of fresh, canned, or frozen fruit, ½ cup of fruit juice
Grains	6	6-8	10-11	1 slice of bread, 1 ounce of dry cereal, 1½ cups of cooked rice, pasta, or cereal
Nuts, legumes, and seeds (per week)	3	4-5	1	1/3 cup or 1 ½ ounces of nuts, 2 Tbsp peanut butter, 2 Tbsp or ½ ounce of seeds, ½ cup of cooked legumes,

				like dried beans or peas
Fats and oils	2	2-3	3	1 tsp of soft margarine, 1 tsp of vegetable oil, 1 Tbsp of mayonnaise, or 2 Tbsp of salad dressing
Sweets and added sugars (per week)	0	5 or less	2 or less	1 Tbsp of sugar, 1 Tbsp jelly or jam, 1½ cups of sorbet or gelatin, or 1 cup of lemonade

Starting the Diet

Before getting started on a new eating program, there are a couple of things you should do. The first, particularly if you have any health issues besides blood pressure, is to visit your doctor. They can advise you on how many calories per day comprise a good intake for you, as well as advising on exercise. It's also important, particularly if you have food allergies or any chronic illnesses, to discuss foods that could be bad for you even if they are part of the DASH diet. For example, if you have a nut or legume allergy, you know to avoid nuts and legumes. But if you have a condition like IBS, there may be other triggers that you aren't aware of yet. A discussion with your doctor can set any fears to rest and help you plan out meals that will work for you as an individual.

The second thing to do before getting started with the DASH diet is to figure out how much you are eating now in terms of calorie intake, and how your intake measures up to your activity level. There are a couple of options for this. One way is to keep a food diary, noting what you eat and how many calories it has, and match it up to an exercise diary where you record your activity.

For a more technology-based approach, you could benefit hugely from downloading an app like My Fitness Pal. Apps like this allow you to document your food and find out how many calories are in each item by checking a database. With My Fitness Pal, you can see how many calories you are taking in, as well as the nutrition balance you are striking between fat, protein, and carbohydrates. This app also allows you to track your exercise and easily calculate how many calories you have burned off. If you want to do more with technology, activity trackers like FitBit record your steps and store data in real time that tells you how many calories you have burned.

Working out what you are consuming and how much you are burning off allows you to pinpoint the aspects of your lifestyle that are most in need of change. From there, you can start making meal plans (more on those later) and swapping out the bad foods in your diet for good ones.

Top Tips for Success

Starting a new diet is always a little daunting, but the DASH diet is too important to be allowed to fall by the wayside. Here are 15 top tips for getting started as you mean to go on.

1. **Go slowly**
   It might seem like jumping in feet first is the way to go, but this isn't some faddy cleanse – it's a complete change in the way you eat, drink, and live day to day. With this in mind, you should give yourself a chance to get used to the changes. Start by changing your dairy products, so you become accustomed to the taste of low fat, and adding more fruit and vegetables to your everyday meals. From there, you can start making

bigger changes one day at a time, like trading fattier cuts of beef for lean meats or changing sugary cereal for oatmeal. Be kind to yourself, and work the changes into your routine gradually. This will make the diet much easier to stick to.

2. **Accept that you're going to be hungry**

   It's awful, but it's true. If you are reducing your calorie intake to, say, 2,000 calories a day from 3,500, you are going to be hungry a lot more. This doesn't mean being paralyzed with starvation for most of the day – that would be unhealthy – it means feeling some nagging dissatisfaction, or the desire to have second helpings you don't actually need. The good news is that the hunger will only last for a few days, and your body will quickly adapt to only consuming what it actually needs.

3. **Take care of your stomach**

   Some people have noticed that the DASH diet causes them a bit of digestive distress at the beginning. This can consist of bloating, diarrhea, or flatulence. This is normal and to be expected when you start taking in much more fiber than you did before. It's also part of the reason it's important to introduce these dietary changes slowly. If you start having trouble, cut down on the amount of green vegetables and fruit you are eating and slowly build them back up. And don't be afraid to visit your doctor and discuss any gastrointestinal issues; stomach health is important!

4. **Make dairy work for you**

   Lactose intolerance is a common problem; it affects 33% of Americans, which totals approximately 40 million people. If you are lactose intolerant, there are ways you can still drink milk and eat yogurt and cheese as part of the DASH diet without getting ill. Supplements like Lactaid are a great help: they provide your body with the enzyme lactase, which is needed to successfully digest dairy products. There are also lactose-free milk and dairy products available in many supermarkets.

If you have a full-blown dairy allergy, all is not lost. Simply substitute the dairy in the diet with soy, coconut, or almond milk. These milks are often fortified with calcium and extra vitamins, so you won't miss out on the nutrients you need. Alternatively, calcium supplements are a great help. Beware of protein powders, though: they are often made with milk. You can get plenty of extra protein from meat and nuts.

5. **Substitute, don't skip**

One of the hardest things for many people to accept about diets is that they are not about self-denial - they are about making changes. If you are craving a snack, then have one! Just make sure it's recommended as part of the DASH diet. Try swapping out chips and fries for popcorn, unsalted pretzels, or carrot sticks. Instead of a creamy dip, try some low-fat hummus (you can make great hummus at home) or peanut butter. There is always a healthy alternative that will satisfy your craving, it's just a matter of finding it.

6. **Find a hobby**

It's very common for people to eat out of boredom, so if it's an issue for you, find a way to occupy yourself. Start a new hobby, ideally one that gets you out of the house and away from the refrigerator. It doesn't have to be expensive or complicated; try going for a few long walks with your phone or camera and taking some pictures, or joining a Meetup group in your area focused on something you're interested in. The less time you spend idle, the less tempted you will be to snack.

7. **Experiment with food**

If you haven't got much experience with cooking, now is the time to start enjoying it. There are all kinds of herbs and spices out there that can really liven up your

DASH-friendly dishes, so pick up a new spice rack and start having some fun!

8. Taste your food before adding salt

This is a very simple tip, but it's hugely important, particularly if you are on the DASH-Sodium diet. It's easy to get into the habit of putting salt and pepper on your food when it isn't needed, so leave those shakers in the cupboard and try eating your food without them for a while.

9. Read the packets

Again, this tip is simple, but it's a useful one. Get into the habit of reading the nutritional information whenever you buy food in a package. Processed foods are full of salt, so if you do find yourself unable to cook one night make sure your ready meal doesn't exceed your salt allowance for the day. When you start reading the packaging on your food, you will be surprised at how much fat and sugar is actually contained in what you eat day to day. It's a great lesson in what foods to avoid!

10. Document what you eat

Don't give up on tools like My Fitness Pal when you start your DASH diet. Keeping track of what you eat and drink lets you know exactly how many calories you have left and how much you are benefiting from your exercise routine. Which brings us to...

11. Start an exercise routine

The NHLBI recommends complementing the diet with some exercise to get the most out of it. They suggest undertaking at least 30 minutes of moderate physical activity almost every day; this will help to burn up calories and improve overall fitness and muscle tone. Try swimming or jogging a few times a week to start you off. Once you get into the habit of exercising, you'll really enjoy it. Exercise will also help to reduce your weight, contributing to better heart health and overall wellbeing.

12. Recruit your family and friends

Obviously, if you're cooking for your family they are going to notice a difference in what's on the table. The DASH diet is great for everyone's health, but if there are other people in the house then there is a good chance they will be eating treats and things that you should avoid. Talk to them about supporting you and not tempting you with goodies, even if it's just during your adjustment period.

Misery loves company, so if you think you're going to be miserable when you start exercising, bring in a friend. If you involve someone else in your routine it will be much harder to avoid exercising. You can also motivate each other, which is extremely helpful if you're feeling low or nervous at the beginning.

13. Try going veggie

It's true that vegetarians and vegans don't necessarily have a healthier diet than carnivores. However, cutting out meat a few days a week will encourage you to eat more vegetables and nuts, thereby building your protein and fiber intake.

14. Invest in a slow cooker

"Invest" may be the wrong word; slow cookers are inexpensive, and they can save you a lot of money in the long run. They are also ideal for making healthy meals without much effort. Want to make a tasty stew? Throw some lean meat, green veggies, and lentils in a slow cooker before you go to work in the morning and turn it to low. When you come home, voila! You'll have a delicious stew that took almost no time to prepare. They are also great for making large amounts of food like chili, Bolognese, or casserole that you can portion up and freeze for later use.

15. Go easy on yourself

Everyone wants to cheat when they make changes to their diet. Even with the knowledge that the DASH diet will lower your blood pressure, it will still be tempting to have that chocolate bar or order that pizza. The key is not to feel bad about it. Don't beat yourself up; just get back on that horse!

Shopping on the DASH Diet

Shopping for food on the DASH diet will take some getting used to, but it's not as difficult as you might think. The main switch to make, if you haven't made it already, is going from processed food to fresh food. This doesn't mean abandoning convenience altogether – there are plenty of canned goods out there that are low in salt and saturated fat, and the same can be said for frozen. It's important to make things as easy for yourself as possible. For example, you can buy in bulk for those days when you plan to make a whole week's worth of meals in one go. If you have plenty of freezer space, healthy frozen food is a great choice. Picking up frozen, pre-prepared fish fillets or chicken breasts is completely fine as long as the packaging doesn't indicate high amounts of salt and fat. It's also worth looking at frozen vegetables, as they will taste just as good as fresh when prepared.

One vital aspect of DASH-friendly shopping is picking up fresh ingredients, or frozen ingredients that come close. A bag of frozen prawns, for example, is quick and easy to defrost and makes a great stir-fry staple. If you're tempted by the thought of pizza, don't buy a frozen one; pick up some wholegrain flour, chicken, vegetables, low-fat cheese, and tomato sauce so you can make your base and toppings from scratch.
Just bear in mind that ingredients are a better choice than full meals, and you won't go wrong. And, as mentioned above, always read the packets!

DASHing Out

Eating out on the DASH diet might seem like a daunting prospect but, again, it's all about changing your habits. The first change is in where you eat. Fast food outlets may claim to offer healthy options now, but their salads can be pretty calorie-filled and the desserts are off the cholesterol charts. If you feel like eating out, investigate the restaurants in your area that offer freshly-made food.

Another concern is what to eat when you actually get out there. Restaurants don't tend to list the calorie content of their meals on the menu, so how will you avoid blowing your diet? Luckily, you can work out what is DASH friendly on the menu simply by using common sense. Stay away from creamy pastas and fatty meats, and look at the chicken and risotto choices instead. It's also important that you aren't afraid to ask questions and make changes. Do you want that salad with a different dressing, or a platter of fruit instead of a pie? Just ask! Most restaurants will take steps to accommodate reasonable requests, and it's good to get into the habit of being consistent with your diet, even if it's a special occasion or you're out as a treat.

One suggestion is to avoid places where there is an expectation that you will eat a lot. Many restaurants are designed to convince you that you need to "get your money's worth", and that's simply not true. If you find yourself at a buffet place, take small portions instead of loading up your plate. You can still make a few trips to the buffet and try everything on offer (as long as it isn't out of bounds on DASH), but you don't have to worry about eating too much.

Chapter Three: Diet Plans

Weekly Plans

Planning out your meals for a week or two in advance is a great way to adapt to the DASH diet. Shopping for food gets a lot easier, as you only have to buy the ingredients you know you will need, and planning meals becomes very simple.

To get you started, we've created two different diet plans, each designed to last for a week. Most of the recipes here can be found later in the book; if not, they are easy to whip up or track down online. Feel free to add your own touches to the recipes, and mix and match from the two plans. Just make sure you stay within the portion guidelines! It's also worth noting that it's absolutely fine to stick with the meals; the snacks are just suggestions to help keep you full all day long.

Diet Plan One - Week One

Monday
Breakfast: Savory Sweet Potato Pancakes
Lunch: Veggie Pasta Salad
Dinner: Easy Veggie Pizza
Snack/Treat: Savory Almonds

Tuesday
Breakfast: Sweet Quinoa
Lunch: Rice, Peas and Shrimp
Dinner: Zucchini and Tomato Pasta Bake
Snack/Treat: Carrot Cake Balls

Wednesday
Breakfast: Glowing Green Morning Smoothie
Lunch: Tuna Mayonnaise Baked Potato
Dinner: Turkey Meatloaf
Snack/Treat: Low Calorie Blueberry Muffins

Thursday
Breakfast: Fruity Oatmeal
Lunch: Easy Chicken Tacos
Dinner: Herb Crusted Cod
Snack/Treat: Sorbet Surprise

Friday
Breakfast: Oaty breakfast Bar
Lunch: Tuna and Spinach Sandwich
Dinner: Veggie Ratatouille
Snack/Treat: Healthy Popsicles

Saturday
Breakfast: Classic Bacon and Eggs
Lunch: Multicolored Chicken Wrap
Dinner: Baked Salmon Fillets
Snack/Treat: Carrot Cake Balls

Sunday
Breakfast: Sweet Quinoa
Lunch: Sausage and Potato Bake
Dinner: Easy Chicken Stir Fry
Snack/Treat: Sweet Dip with Fruit and Crackers

Diet Plan One - Week Two

Monday
Breakfast: Green Smoothie
Lunch: Veggie Pasta Salad
Dinner: Zucchini Spaghetti Bolognese
Snack/Treat: Fruit Salad

Tuesday
Breakfast: Classic Bacon and Eggs
Lunch: Zesty Quinoa
Dinner: Turkey Meatloaf
Snack/Treat: Low Calorie Blueberry Muffins

Wednesday
Breakfast: Orange Morning Smoothie
Lunch: Multicolored Chicken Wrap
Dinner: Zucchini and Tomato Pasta Bake
Snack/Treat: Savory Almonds

Thursday
Breakfast: Fruit Salad with a sprinkle of Cinnamon
Lunch: Easy Chicken Tacos
Dinner: Turkey Meatloaf
Snack/Treat: Sorbet Surprise

Friday
Breakfast: Fruity Oatmeal
Lunch: Rice, Peas and Shrimp
Dinner: Herb Crusted Cod
Snack/Treat: Healthy Popsicles

Saturday
Breakfast: Scrambled Spanish Eggs
Lunch: Crockpot Beans and Rice
Dinner: Easy Veggie Pizza
Snack/Treat: Nutty Berry Smoothie

Sunday

Breakfast: Orange Morning Smoothie
Lunch: Salmon and Vegetable Pita
Dinner: Steak and Sweet Potato Fries
Snack/Treat: No-Coffee Iced Coffee

Diet Plan One - Week Three

Monday
Breakfast: Sweet Quinoa
Lunch: Zesty Quinoa
Dinner: Slow Roasted Chicken
Snack/Treat: No-Coffee Iced Coffee

Tuesday
Breakfast: Oaty Breakfast Bars
Lunch: Tuna Mayonnaise Baked Potato
Dinner: Steak and Sweet Potato Fries
Snack/Treat: Nutty Berry Smoothie

Wednesday
Breakfast: Orange Morning Smoothie
Lunch: Easy Chicken Tacos
Dinner: Baked Salmon Fillets
Snack/Treat: Sorbet Surprise

Thursday
Breakfast: Scrambled Spanish Eggs
Lunch: Salmon and Vegetable Pita
Dinner: Easy Chicken Stir Fry
Snack/Treat: Healthy Popsicles

Friday
Breakfast: Avocado, Banana and Chocolate Smoothie
Lunch: Veggie Pasta Salad
Dinner: Easy Veggie Pizza
Snack/Treat: Savory Almonds

Saturday
Breakfast: Old Fashioned Corn Muffins
Lunch: Tuna and Spinach Sandwich
Dinner: Veggie Ratatouille
Snack/Treat: Fruit and Crackers with a Sweet Dip

Sunday
Breakfast: Fruity Oatmeal
Lunch: Multicolored Chicken Wrap
Dinner: Zucchini Spaghetti Bolognese
Snack/Treat: Low Calorie Blueberry Muffins

Diet Plan One - Week Four

Monday
Breakfast: Savory Sweet Potato Pancakes
Lunch: Rice, Peas and Shrimp
Dinner: Zucchini and Tomato Pasta Bake
Snack/Treat: Carrot Cake Balls

Tuesday
Breakfast: Glowing Green Morning Smoothie
Lunch: Crockpot Beans and Rice
Dinner: Turkey Meatloaf
Snack/Treat: Low Fat Hummus with Chips

Wednesday
Breakfast: Classic Bacon and Eggs
Lunch: Sausage and Potato Bake
Dinner: Herb Crusted Cod
Snack/Treat: Low Calorie Blueberry Muffins

Thursday
Breakfast: Fruity Oatmeal
Lunch: Multicolored Chicken Wrap
Dinner: Zucchini Spaghetti Bolognese
Snack/Treat: Fruit and Crackers with a Sweet Dip

Friday
Breakfast: Old Fashioned Corn Muffins
Lunch: Tuna and Spinach Salad
Dinner: Veggie Ratatouille
Snack/Treat: Savory Almonds

Saturday
Breakfast: Avocado, Banana and Chocolate Smoothie
Lunch: Veggie Pasta Salad
Dinner: Easy Veggie Pizza
Snack/Treat: Healthy Popsicles

Sunday
Breakfast: Scrambled Spanish Eggs
Lunch: Salmon and Vegetable Pita
Dinner: Easy Chicken Stir-Fry
Snack/Treat: Sorbet Surprise

Diet Plan Two - Week One

Monday
Breakfast: Oaty Breakfast Bars
Lunch: Veggie Pasta Salad
Dinner: Zucchini Spaghetti Bolognese
Snack/Treat: Fruit Salad

Tuesday
Breakfast: Classic Bacon and Eggs
Lunch: Veggie Pasta Salad
Dinner: Turkey Meatloaf
Snack/Treat: Low Calorie Blueberry Muffins

Wednesday
Breakfast: Orange Morning Smoothie
Lunch: Multicolored Chicken Wrap
Dinner: Zucchini and Tomato Pasta Bake
Snack/Treat: Savory Almonds

Thursday
Breakfast: Fruit Salad with a sprinkle of Cinnamon
Lunch: Easy Chicken Tacos
Dinner: Turkey Meatloaf
Snack/Treat: Sorbet Surprise

Friday
Breakfast: Fruity Oatmeal
Lunch: Rice, Peas and Shrimp
Dinner: Herb Crusted Cod
Snack/Treat: Healthy Popsicles

Saturday
Breakfast: Scrambled Spanish Eggs
Lunch: Crockpot Beans and Rice
Dinner: Easy Veggie Pizza
Snack/Treat: Nutty Berry Smoothie

Sunday
Breakfast: Orange Morning Smoothie
Lunch: Salmon and Vegetable Pita
Dinner: Steak and Sweet Potato Fries
Snack/Treat: No-Coffee Iced Coffee

Diet Plan Two - Week Two

Monday
Breakfast: Glowing Green Morning Smoothie
Lunch: Zesty Quinoa
Dinner: Slow Roasted Chicken
Snack/Treat: No-Coffee Iced Coffee

Tuesday
Breakfast: Oaty Breakfast Bars
Lunch: Rice, Peas and Shrimp
Dinner: Steak and Sweet Potato Fries
Snack/Treat: Nutty Berry Smoothie

Wednesday
Breakfast: Orange Morning Smoothie
Lunch: Easy Chicken Tacos
Dinner: Baked Salmon Fillets
Snack/Treat: Sorbet Surprise

Thursday
Breakfast: Scrambled Spanish Eggs
Lunch: Salmon and Vegetable Pita
Dinner: Easy Chicken Stir Fry
Snack/Treat: Healthy Popsicles

Friday
Breakfast: Orange Morning Smoothie
Lunch: Veggie Pasta Salad
Dinner: Easy Veggie Pizza
Snack/Treat: Savory Almonds

Saturday
Breakfast: Old Fashioned Corn Muffins
Lunch: Tuna and Spinach Sandwich
Dinner: Veggie Ratatouille
Snack/Treat: Fruit and Crackers with a Sweet Dip

Sunday
Breakfast: Fruity Oatmeal
Lunch: Multicolored Chicken Wrap
Dinner: Zucchini Spaghetti Bolognese
Snack/Treat: Low Calorie Blueberry Muffins

Diet Plan Two - Week Three

Monday
Breakfast: Savory Sweet Potato Pancakes
Lunch: Rice, Peas and Shrimp
Dinner: Zucchini and Tomato Pasta Bake
Snack/Treat: Carrot Cake Balls

Tuesday
Breakfast: Glowing Green Morning Smoothie
Lunch: Crockpot Beans and Rice
Dinner: Turkey Meatloaf
Snack/Treat: Low Fat Hummus with Chips

Wednesday
Breakfast: Classic Bacon and Eggs
Lunch: Sausage and Potato Bake
Dinner: Herb Crusted Cod
Snack/Treat: Low Calorie Blueberry Muffins

Thursday
Breakfast: Fruity Oatmeal
Lunch: Multicolored Chicken Wrap
Dinner: Zucchini Spaghetti Bolognese
Snack/Treat: Fruit and Crackers with a Sweet Dip

Friday
Breakfast: Old Fashioned Corn Muffins
Lunch: Tuna and Spinach Salad
Dinner: Veggie Ratatouille
Snack/Treat: Savory Almonds

Saturday
Breakfast: Avocado, Banana and Chocolate Smoothie
Lunch: Veggie Pasta Salad
Dinner: Easy Veggie Pizza
Snack/Treat: Healthy Popsicles

Sunday

Breakfast: Scrambled Spanish Eggs
Lunch: Salmon and Vegetable Pita
Dinner: Easy Chicken Stir-Fry
Snack/Treat: Sorbet Surprise

Diet Plan Two - Week Four

Monday
Breakfast: Sweet Quinoa
Lunch: Veggie Pasta Salad
Dinner: Easy Veggie Pizza
Snack/Treat: Savory Almonds

Tuesday
Breakfast: Sweet Quinoa
Lunch: Rice, Peas and Shrimp
Dinner: Zucchini and Tomato Pasta Bake
Snack/Treat: Carrot Cake Balls

Wednesday
Breakfast: Glowing Green Morning Smoothie
Lunch: Tuna Mayonnaise Baked Potato
Dinner: Turkey Meatloaf
Snack/Treat: Low Calorie Blueberry Muffins

Thursday
Breakfast: Fruity Oatmeal
Lunch: Easy Chicken Tacos
Dinner: Crockpot Beans and Rice
Snack/Treat: Sorbet Surprise

Friday
Breakfast: Oaty breakfast Bar
Lunch: Tuna and Spinach Sandwich
Dinner: Veggie Ratatouille
Snack/Treat: Healthy Popsicles

Saturday
Breakfast: Classic Bacon and Eggs
Lunch: Multicolored Chicken Wrap
Dinner: Baked Salmon Fillets
Snack/Treat: Carrot Cake Balls

Sunday
Breakfast: Sweet Quinoa
Lunch: Sausage and Potato Bake
Dinner: Easy Chicken Stir Fry
Snack/Treat: Sweet Dip with Fruit and Crackers

Chapter Four: Breakfast

Starting your day right is the key to success with any diet or meal plan. To help you get going, here are ten fantastic breakfast recipes that you can enjoy without worrying about your diet. Feel free to mix them up and add your own personal touches as far as the diet allows.

Savory Sweet Potato Pancakes

Ingredients
- 4 cups of sweet potato, grated
- ½ a small brown onion, finely chopped
- ¼ cup of spelt flour
- Pinch of salt and pepper
- 1 beaten egg
- A drizzle of canola oil (olive or corn oil is fine too)

Instructions
Drizzle the oil into a non-stick frying pan or skillet and heat up the pan while mixing the other ingredients together thoroughly. When the oil is hot, spoon out the mixture a ¼ cup at a time into the pan and flatten it out until each cake is around an inch thick. Cook until golden brown on each side and serve.

Glowing Green Morning Smoothie

Ingredients
- 1 cup baby spinach
- 1 banana
- ¼ cup oats, whole
- ¾ cup mango
- ¼ cup fat free plain yogurt
- ½ cup skim milk (coconut or soy milk works too)
- ¼ chopped apple

Instructions
Start by blending the oats, milk, and yogurt at the highest setting until it's all smooth. Then add the other ingredients and blend until it's thick but all the lumps are gone. When you're happy with the texture, pour into a glass and enjoy!

Classic Bacon and Eggs

Ingredients
- 3 large free range eggs
- Splash or skim or coconut milk
- 2 slices of bacon
- Sprinkling of chives

Instructions
Trim the fat from the bacon and place it under the grill. While cooking, dab it with a paper towel now and again to remove excess grease. Meanwhile, scramble the eggs, adding the milk for extra flavor. When the bacon is done, chop it up and mix it in with the eggs. Add the chives, stir, and serve.

Fruity Oatmeal

Ingredients
- ½ cup oatmeal
- ½ cup skim milk (or coconut milk)
- 1 cup strawberries
- 1 small banana

Instructions
Make the oatmeal using the milk. While it's still hot, stir in the strawberries and banana, and serve.

Old-Fashioned Corn Muffins

Ingredients

- 1 cup flour
- 1 cup skim milk
- 1 egg
- ¼ cup sugar
- 1 ¼ cups cornmeal, ideally stone-ground
- 1 cup corn
- ½ bell pepper
- 2 tsp baking powder
- 4 Tbsp melted margarine

Instructions

Add the dry ingredients to a large bowl and mix together. Use another bowl to mix the milk, margarine, egg, corn, cornmeal, and pepper. Combine with the dry ingredients and blend together until the mixture is only a little lumpy. Heat your oven to 400F and prepare a muffin pan with liners, then spoon the mix into the cups until they are two-thirds full. Bake the muffins for 20-25 minutes and make sure they are golden brown. Remove from the oven and wait five minutes, then put them on a wire rack to cool before serving.

Avocado, Banana, and Chocolate Smoothie

Ingredients
- 2 cups vanilla soy milk, almond milk, or Rice Dream
- ½ a prepared avocado
- 1 chopped banana
- ¼ cup unsweetened cocoa powder
- 1 tsp sugar

Instructions
Mix all the ingredients together in a blender and blend at high speed until smooth. For a thicker smoothie, try fat-free vanilla or plain yogurt instead of milk.

Scrambled Spanish Eggs

Ingredients
- 3 eggs
- 1 ½ cups egg substitute
- ¼ cup skim milk
- ¾ cup chopped tomatoes
- ¼ cup chopped red pepper
- ¼ cup diced onion
- Sprinkling of salt and pepper
- 1/4 teaspoon tabasco sauce (to taste, use more or less if you like!)
- A drizzle of canola or olive oil

Instructions
Heat up a frying pan and drizzle the oil into it. Add the tomato, onions, and pepper and heat until they've softened up. Take them out of the pan. Mix the eggs, egg substitute, milk, salt, pepper, and tabasco in a bowl and beat with a whisk until they're properly blended. Pour the mixture into the pan and turn down the heat, then stir like you're making scrambled eggs. Cook until the eggs are scrambled then add the tomato, pepper, and onions again and mix together before serving.

Orange Morning Smoothie

Ingredients
- 1 cup vanilla fat-free yogurt
- ¾ cup skim milk
- ½ cup fresh orange juice

Instructions
Blend the ingredients together until smooth and serve right away.

Oaty Breakfast Bars

Ingredients
- 2 ½ cups rolled oats
- ½ cup wheat germ, toasted
- ½ cup powdered fat-free milk
- ½ cup soy flour
- ½ cup chopped toasted pecans
- ½ cup raisins
- ½ cup dried pears
- ½ cup peanut butter
- 1 cup honey
- ½ tsp salt
- 2 tsp vanilla extract

Instructions
1 Tbsp olive oil, plus another drizzle for preparation

Drizzle olive oil on a large baking pan and preheat oven to 325F. Then thoroughly mix the dry milk, flour, wheat germ, oats, nuts, fruit, and salt in a large bowl.

Heat the peanut butter, honey, and olive oil in a small saucepan over a low heat until it is fully combined before adding the vanilla. Mix this into the large bowl with the dry ingredients and stir briskly until the mixture is firm and sticky.

Place the mixture in the pan, making sure not to create air pockets, and bake for 25 minutes. Remove the pan from the oven and allow it to cool for 10-15 minutes before cutting it into bars (you can make 24 from this amount). Take the bars out of the pan and cool on a wire rack. It's best to store the bars in Tupperware in your refrigerator. Have one bar at a time for breakfast.

Sweet Quinoa

Ingredients
- 1 cup fresh quinoa
- 2 cups skim milk
- ¼ cup honey
- ¼ cup sliced almonds
- ¼ cup raisins
- ¼ tsp cinnamon (add more if you like!)

Instructions
Make sure the quinoa is rinsed, and then boil the milk in a pan. Reduce the heat, add the quinoa, and bring to a boil again. Simmer until the milk is mostly absorbed, which should take around 15 minutes on a low heat. When the milk is gone, take it off the heat and fluff the quinoa with a fork. Stir in the other ingredients and cover the pan, then leave it to stand for 15 minutes before serving.

Chapter Five: Lunch

Even when you're having a busy day, it's important to make time for lunch. Here are ten great recipes you can prepare quickly at home or take with you to work. The important thing is staying full all day so you aren't tempted by unhealthy snacks!

Some of these will make a few servings, but everything is suitable for refrigeration so you can prep your lunch for a few days in one go.

Rice, Peas, and Shrimp

Ingredients
- 8 oz prepared medium shrimp
- 1 cup brown rice
- 2/3 of a cup frozen peas
- 3 minced garlic cloves
- 1 Tbsp white wine vinegar
- Sprinkling of salt and red pepper
- ¼ tsp ground turmeric
- 2 Tbsp chopped parsley
- ¼ cup water
- A drizzle of olive oil

Instructions
Prepare the rice and set it aside. Heat the oil in a frying pan and add the shrimp. Sauté the shrimp for two minutes then add the garlic to the pan and heat for another minute. Heat a pan of water until it is simmering and cook the peas for around two minutes. Drain the pan and add the shrimp and rice. Mix the vinegar, turmeric, salt, and red pepper and cook together for another minute or two. Serve and season with parsley.

Crockpot Beans and Rice

Ingredients
- 1 ½ cups brown rice
- 15 oz garbanzo beans
- 15 oz dark kidney beans
- 3 cups water
- ¼ cup olive oil
- 1/3 cup rice vinegar
- ½ cup chopped shallots
- ½ cup chopped parsley

Instructions
Rinse the rice and put it in a crockpot with the water. Cook on a medium heat for 50 minutes, and give it longer if the rice isn't tender enough or the water isn't completely absorbed. Let it cool then stir in the remaining ingredients. Leave it to cool then place in the refrigerator for two hours to chill fully.

Sausage and Potato Bake

Ingredients
- ½ pound smoked turkey sausage
- 1 pound potatoes, skin on
- 2 medium brown onions
- 1 tsp crushed, dried thyme
- 2 tsps cumin
- Olive oil for cooking
- Pinch of salt and pepper

Instructions
Cook sausage and set it aside. Cut the potatoes into cubes and the onions into thin slices. Cover the bottom of a skillet with the olive oil and place over medium heat. Simmer the potatoes and onions in the oil for 12-15 minutes, until the potatoes are almost softened. Slice the sausage into thin, diagonal pieces and add it to the potatoes, then cook it all together for 10-12 minutes. Stir in the thyme and cumin and add salt and pepper to taste, and then stir to ensure it's all fully mixed before serving.

Multicolored Chicken Wrap

Ingredients
- 1 large chicken breast
- 1 large whole wheat tortilla
- 4 large lettuce leaves
- 2/3 cup drained canned mandarin oranges
- 1/3 cup diced celery
- ¼ cup minced brown onion
- 2 Tbsp low fat mayonnaise
- 1 tsp low sodium soy sauce
- ¼ tsp garlic powder
- Sprinkling of black pepper
- Drizzle olive oil

Instructions
Add the olive oil to a frying pan, cut the chicken into strips, and cook the chicken fully. Allow it to cool then mix it in a bowl with the onion, oranges, and celery. Mix the soy sauce, mayonnaise, garlic, and pepper together and add them to the bowl. Make sure the chicken is fully coated in the other ingredients. Cut the tortilla into four quarters and lay out one lettuce leaf on each one. Split the chicken mixture into four and add it to the quarters, then roll the wraps into cones and serve.

Tuna and Spinach Sandwich Filling

Ingredients
- 6 oz of tuna
- 1 cup baby spinach
- ½ diced medium cucumber
- ½ diced small red onion
- ½ cup diced celery
- ½ tsp dill weed
- Pinch of oregano
- A drizzle of olive oil
- A drizzle of lemon juice
- Pinch of black pepper

Instructions
Mix the tuna with the onion, cucumber, dill weed, and celery. Drizzle on the olive oil and lemon juice, to taste, and stir. Add the oregano and pepper and mix with the spinach before serving. You will get four or five sandwiches out of this amount of mix.

Veggie Pasta Salad

Ingredients
- 12 oz whole wheat pasta
- 1 pound sliced mushrooms
- 2 medium shredded zucchini
- 2 chopped brown onions
- 2 sliced bell peppers
- 28 oz diced tomatoes
- 8 lettuce leaves
- ¼ cup low-salt vegetable broth
- 1 tsp minced garlic
- Pinch of oregano
- Pinch of basil

Instructions
Make and drain the pasta, then toss with the olive oil. Put the broth in a skillet or large frying pan over a medium heat and add the garlic, tomatoes, and onions. Heat them for about five minutes before adding the peppers, zucchini, and mushrooms, then sauté all together for 5-7 minutes. Add the basil and oregano to taste. Mix the sauce together with the pasta and mix together, then refrigerate under a cover until chilled. To serve, place the lettuce leaves on plates and spoon out the pasta.

Salmon and Vegetable Pita

Ingredients
- ¾ cup of salmon, cubed
- 3 whole wheat pitas
- 3 lettuce leaves
- 3 Tbsp fat-free plain yogurt
- 2 Tbsp shredded bell pepper
- 1 Tbsp lemon juice
- 1 tsp capers
- Pinch of dill
- Pinch of black pepper

Instructions
Chop the capers and mix the yogurt, salmon, pepper, lemon juice, and capers together. Add the dill and pepper to taste. Line the pitas with one lettuce leaf each and spoon the salmon mix inside each one, around 1/3 of a cup per pita.

Easy Chicken Tacos

Ingredients
- 1/3 cup cubed chicken breast
- 2 taco shells
- 2 Tbsp chopped celery
- 1 Tbsp light mayonnaise
- 1 tablespoon salsa
- 1 tablespoon grated cheese
- A drizzle of olive or canola oil

Instructions
Add the oil to a frying pan and cook the chicken over a medium heat. Set it aside to cool and mix the celery, salsa, and mayonnaise together. When the chicken has cooled, mix it in and spoon into the taco shells. Sprinkle the cheese on top and serve.

Tuna Mayonnaise Baked Potato

Ingredients
- 1 large potato
- 2/3 cup tuna, drained
- 2 Tbsp low fat mayonnaise
- Sprinkling of parsley

Instructions
Pierce the skin on the potato and place it in the microwave for five minutes at full power. Turn the potato over and place it in for another five minutes. Mix the tuna and mayonnaise together. Slice the potato in two and add the tuna mix, then sprinkle with parsley.

Zesty Quinoa

Ingredients
- ½ cup fresh quinoa
- 1 cup diced cucumber
- ½ cup sliced cherry tomatoes
- 1/8 cup feta cheese, crumbled
- 1 Tbsp olive oil
- ½ squeezed lemon
- 1/8 cup diced red onion
- 5 prepared kalamata olives
- Pinch of black pepper

Instructions
Rinse the quinoa thoroughly and place in a medium-sized pot full of water. Boil the water, then turn down the heat and simmer for 15 minutes. Turn off the heat, allow to cool, then fluff the quinoa with a fork before adding the cucumber, tomatoes, onion, and olives. Drizzle the olive oil and lemon juice over the top, then add the feta cheese and mix in. Season everything with black pepper to taste before serving.

Chapter Six: Dinner

Preparing dinner can be a real chore, especially if you have a family who all want to eat too! Luckily, we have ten delicious dinner recipes that everyone will love.

Zucchini and Tomato Pasta Bake

Ingredients
- 1½ cups whole wheat penne pasta
- 1 ½ cups cubed zucchini
- 2 ½ cups low-salt tomato sauce
- 1 cup grated low-fat mozzarella
- ¼ cup grated Parmesan
- ¼ cup chopped brown onion
- 1 garlic clove
- 2 tsp oregano
- 2 tsp basil
- Pinch of black pepper
- Drizzle of canola oil

Instructions
Cook the pasta for five minutes, to make sure it softens slightly, and drain it. Spread the canola oil over a large casserole dish and preheat your oven to 350F. Set aside half of the mozzarella and Parmesan for the topping. Mix the tomato sauce with the basil, onion, oregano, and pepper, then crush the garlic clove and add this too. Mix well and add the zucchini, then mix in the rest of the mozzarella and Parmesan. Finally add the pasta and place in the dish. Top with the remaining cheese and bake for 25-30 minutes. This dish typically serves six.

Turkey Meatloaf

Ingredients
- 1 pound lean turkey, ground
- ½ cup oats
- 1 large egg
- 1 Tbsp dehydrated onion flakes
- ¼ cup low-salt ketchup

Instructions
Preheat your oven to 350F. Mix all ingredients together, making sure they are properly combined. Place the mixture in a loaf tin and bake for 25-30 minutes. Serve with salad or boiled potatoes. This should serve five people.

Herb-Crusted Cod

Ingredients
- 4 cod fillets weighing 4oz each
- ¾ cup herb stuffing
- ¼ cup honey
- A drizzle of olive oil
- ½ a lemon

Instructions
Place the stuffing in a Ziploc bag and use a rolling pin to crush it into crumbs. Preheat your oven to 375F. Use a brush to lightly coat the cod fillets with honey and cover them with the stuffing crumbs. Coat them thickly (you can even put them in the Ziploc bag to do this). Drizzle the olive oil on the bottom of a baking pan and smooth it out so it is completely covered, then place the fillets on the pan. Bake the fish for ten minutes, until it is cooked all the way through. Squeeze the lemon over the top of the fillets for extra flavor and serve with salad or new potatoes. This dish serves four people, but you can add more honey and stuffing if you are serving more than four fillets.

Zucchini Spaghetti Bolognese

Ingredients
- 2 large zucchini
- 6 oz lean ground beef
- 1 jar low-salt tomato sauce
- 5 chestnut mushrooms
- 2 chopped bell peppers
- 1 crushed garlic clove
- A drizzle of olive oil

Instructions
Start by preparing the zucchini. Use a julienne peeler to strip the zucchini into long, thin strips. Set them aside and brown the beef for around 5 minutes, until it is cooked thoroughly, and drain any excess liquid or fat. Put the zucchini spaghetti in a pan of water to boil, just like pasta, for around 3-5 minutes. Drizzle a separate frying pan with the oil and sauté the peppers for 3 minutes, then add the mushrooms and garlic and continue to heat for another 3-5 minutes. Add the tomato sauce to the beef and allow it to heat up before adding the vegetables and stirring it all together. Drain the zucchini pasta and serve. This dish serves two.

Veggie Ratatouille

Ingredients
- ½ pound whole wheat pasta
- ½ cup Swiss cheese
- 1 small brown onion
- 1 red bell pepper
- 2 zucchini
- 1 eggplant
- 2 tomatoes
- 1 garlic clove
- 5 chestnut mushrooms
- A drizzle of olive oil
- Pinch of basil
- Pinch of salt and pepper

Instructions
Chop the vegetables into cubes and crush the garlic clove. Drizzle oil into a frying pan and heat the pepper and eggplant for 5 minutes. Add the onion, mushrooms, zucchini, and garlic and heat for another 10 minutes. While you heat those, add the pasta to a pot of boiling water and simmer for 10-12 minutes. When the pasta is done, set it aside and add the basil, salt, and pepper to the vegetables and cook for another 2 minutes. Drain the pasta and serve the sauce on top. Sprinkle with the Swiss cheese. This meal serves six people.

Easy Veggie Pizza

Ingredients
- 1 ball of premade whole grain pizza dough
- 2 oz low-fat mozzarella
- 2 ½ cups tomatoes, sliced
- ½ cup baby spinach
- 1 bell pepper
- 1 Tbsp minced oregano
- 1 Tbsp minced garlic
- Pinch of flaked chilies
- Sprinkling of plain flour
- Drizzle of olive oil

Instructions
Chop the pepper and heat it in the pan with the olive oil for a few minutes until it softens, and set it aside. Sprinkle flour on the counter and roll out the pizza dough until it is about a ¼ inch thick. Preheat the oven to 450F and place the dough on a flat baking pan. Shred the mozzarella, then place the tomatoes on the dough and sprinkle the mozzarella on top. Add the peppers, spinach, garlic, oregano, and chilies. Spread everything out evenly, making sure the dough is fully covered. Place the pizza in the oven for 12 minutes, rotating halfway through. This pizza usually serves six.

Easy Chicken Stir-Fry

Ingredients
- 2 cups of chicken breast, cut into strips
- 3 cups brown rice
- ½ cup chopped celery
- ½ cup chopped mushrooms
- ½ cup water chestnuts
- ½ cup cashew nuts
- ¼ cup snow peas
- 1 Tbsp olive or canola oil
- 1 Tbsp low-salt soy sauce (avoid this ingredient on DASH-Sodium)

Instructions
Rinse the rice and add it to a pot of boiling water. Let it simmer for 30 minutes before starting on the rest. Heat the oil in a wok and add the chicken. Cook for 5-7 minutes until cooked through, then add the chestnuts, cashew nuts, mushrooms, celery, and snow peas. Cook for another five minutes and add the soy sauce. Cook it all together for another 2 minutes, then remove from the heat. Drain the rice and serve. This should serve 6-8 people.

Baked Salmon Fillets

Ingredients
- 4 salmon fillets, 6 oz each
- 4 cloves of garlic
- ¼ cup minced dill
- 1 lemon
- Drizzle of olive oil
- Pinch of black pepper

Instructions
Drizzle the oil onto the bottom of a glass baking dish and preheat your oven to 400F. Peel and mince the garlic cloves and cut the lemon into four quarters. Squeeze lemon juice over each fillet, and then lightly coat the fillets with dill and black pepper. Bake the salmon for 22 minutes. This dish serves four people, and is great with salad, brown rice, or new potatoes.

Steak and Sweet Potato Fries

Ingredients
- 1 large sweet potato
- 2 lean sirloin steaks
- 1 tsp mixed herbs
- Drizzle of olive oil
- Pinch of cornflour

Instructions
Preheat your oven to 400F. Scrub the sweet potato and cut into thin fries. Drizzle the oil onto a flat baking pan, making sure it is covered in a thin layer, and place the fries on it, dabbing them with a paper towel to remove excess moisture. Sprinkle a pinch of cornflour over the fries to absorb excess water while cooking. Place in the oven for 10 minutes, then turn them and place back in for 5-10 minutes. Add olive oil to a frying pan and heat it up, then trim any fat from the steaks and coat both sides with mixed herbs for flavor. Heat the steaks for two minutes on each side (or longer, depending on thickness and your preferences). Take the fries out of the oven and serve immediately. This dish serves two.

Slow-Roasted Chicken

Ingredients
- 1 medium chicken
- 1 lemon
- 2 garlic cloves
- 1 brown onion
- 2 tsp mixed herbs

Instructions
Chop the lemon and the onion into quarters and separate the garlic cloves. Lay them on the bottom of your slow cooker. Prep the chicken (remove giblets, etc) and place on the bed of lemon, onion, and garlic. Sprinkle the mixed herbs over the top of the chicken and close the lid. Set the slow cooker to Low for six hours, and then test with a meat thermometer. It should have an internal temperature of 165F. This serves at least three people.

Chapter 7: Snacks and Treats

Even the most resolute dieter knows that it's okay to have an occasional treat. Luckily, it's possible to enjoy treats on the DASH diet without worrying about having too many portions or eating something that doesn't fit. To get you started, here are ten recipes for various snacks you can enjoy without worrying about too much fat or salt.

Carrot Cake Balls

Ingredients
- ½ cup no-salt peanut butter
- 1 cup grated carrot
- ½ cup raisins
- 1/3 cup flaxseed
- ½ a lemon
- Drizzle of honey

Instructions
Mix all the ingredients together in a bowl, then scoop out balls with an ice cream scoop and shape them. Place in the refrigerator for 45 minutes to chill and enjoy! This makes 8-10 balls.

Low-Fat Hummus

Ingredients
- 1 can of chickpeas
- 2 Tbsp sesame seed paste
- 1 garlic clove
- ¼ cup olive oil
- 1 tsp ground cumin
- Pinch of salt

Instructions
Mix everything together and blend at high speed in a blender. Check the consistency and add a tablespoon of water any time it seems too thick. When you have a smooth and creamy mixture, your hummus is ready. Serve with crudités, low-salt tortilla chips, crackers, or anything you like!

Low-Fat Guacamole

Ingredients
- 3 avocados
- 1 large tomato
- 1 red onion
- 1 chili
- ¼ cup coriander leaves
- 1 Tbsp lime juice

Instructions
Start by chopping the coriander leaves, the onion, and the chili, making sure to remove all the seeds from the latter. Then pulverize the tomato and place it in a bowl. Slice the avocados in half and remove the stones, setting one stone aside. Remove the avocado flesh and put it in the bowl with the tomato, and mix them together. Add the onion, chili, coriander, and lime juice and mix together thoroughly. If you are planning to save the guacamole, place an avocado stone in the mix to keep it from turning brown. Serve with low-salt tortilla chips.

Low-Calorie Blueberry Muffins

Ingredients
- 1 ½ cups whole-wheat flour
- 1 cup skim milk
- 1 egg
- 2/3 cup frozen blueberries
- ½ cup oats
- 1/3 cup sugar (or sugar substitute)
- ½ cup low-fat powdered milk
- ¼ cup canola oil
- ½ tsp baking powder
- ¼ tsp baking soda
- ½ tsp salt

Instructions
Line a muffin tin with margarine and preheat your oven to 350F. Mix the flour, sugar, oatmeal, baking soda, baking powder, and salt in one bowl, and the milk, oil, egg, and dry milk in a second bowl. Make sure they are thoroughly combined, then fold the bowl with the milk into the other bowl and add the blueberries. Stir a few times until there is a lumpy mixture, and spoon it into the muffin tray. Fill each muffin section 2/3 high. Bake the muffins for 20 minutes and allow them to cool on a wire rack. This recipe makes around 12 muffins.

Sweet Dip for Fruit and Crackers

Ingredients
- 8 oz fat-free cream cheese, softened
- 2 Tbsp peanuts, chopped
- 2 Tbsp brown sugar
- 1 ½ tsp vanilla

Instructions
Mix the cream cheese with the sugar and vanilla until thoroughly combined, then add the peanuts. This is great for a low fat sweet treat.

Savory Almonds

Ingredients
- 10 oz whole almonds
- 1 Tbsp fresh rosemary
- 1 Tbsp olive oil
- 1 tsp salt
- Pinch of red pepper

Instructions
Chop the rosemary finely, then preheat your oven to 325F and line a flat baking tray with foil. Mix everything together in a bowl, ensuring the almonds are completely coated. Lay the almonds on the baking tray, making sure none of them are overlapping. Bake for 20 minutes and serve.

Healthy Popsicles

Ingredients
- 1 cup orange juice
- 1 cup chopped strawberries
- ½ cup mango juice
- 1 medium banana

Instructions
Cut the banana into small pieces and combine all the ingredients in a blender. Mix until smooth, then pour into individual lolly molds and freeze for 4 hours.

Sorbet Surprise

Ingredients
- ½ cup low-fat orange sorbet
- ½ cup low-fat mango sorbet
- ¼ cup chopped strawberries
- ¼ cup cubed pineapple
- Low-fat whipped cream
- 1 glacé cherry

Instructions
Take two sundae glasses and layer the orange sorbet, pineapple, mango sorbet, and pineapple. Top with whipped cream and the cherry. This is a great dessert for two, but you can always have one to yourself!

Nutty Berry Smoothie

Ingredients
- 1 cup frozen raspberries
- 1 Tbsp no-salt peanut butter
- ½ a ripe banana
- ¼ cup skim or coconut milk

Instructions
Put all the ingredients in a blender and blend until it's smooth and creamy. Add some ice water before blending if you want to thin it out and cool it down.

No-Coffee Iced Coffee

Ingredients
- 2/3 cup skim or coconut milk
- 2 tsp powdered chicory
- 2 tsp honey
- ½ cup crushed ice

Instructions
Add the chicory to the milk and mix until it has dissolved. Add the honey and ice and blend until liquid. Serve over more ice for a cool treat!

Conclusion

So let's review what we know so far. The DASH and DASH-Sodium diets are designed to ensure you consume a healthy amount of nutrients and vitamins and lower your blood pressure in the process. The diet works best as part of a lifestyle change, so it's best to start an exercise regime and consider cutting back on other vices (like alcohol and smoking).

This may seem like a dizzying array of changes, and that can be hard to cope with. But in reality, changing a few small things makes it much easier to alter the big things. Start with altering your routine slightly: cycle to the store instead of driving, for example, or try one of the DASH-friendly recipes in this book. After that it will seem easier to make substantial changes, such as downloading a fitness app or trying a week of DASH meals.

It's important to remember that a good diet isn't a temporary thing: it's a change in the way you eat, drink, get active, and generally live your life. If your health permits it, you can make exercise part of your daily routine. And changing what you eat becomes second nature after a while. You may think that the day you turn down a bag of chips and eat an apple will never come, but it will! Your body's tastes will change and so will yours.

Of course, above all else, it's vital to take care of your health. Make sure you are eating enough calories every day, and don't miss meals or go hungry in the hope you will lose weight faster. Long-lasting weight loss and lower blood pressure do take time to achieve, and that's okay.

If you have any concerns about the diet or your lifestyle in general, talk to your doctor. They can advise you on how to fit the diet into your life and exercise in a way that works for you.

Happy DASHing!

Free Ebook Offer
The Ultimate Guide To Vitamins

I'm very excited to be able to make this offer to you. This is a wonderful 10k word ebook that has been made available to you through my publisher, Valerian Press. As a health conscious person you should be well aware of the uses and health benefits of each of the vitamins that should make up our diet. This book gives you an easy to understand, scientific explanation of the vitamin followed by the recommended daily dosage. It then highlights all the important health benefits of each vitamin. A list of the best sources of each vitamin is provided and you are also given some actionable next steps for each vitamin to make sure you are utilizing the information!

As well as receiving the free ebooks you will also be sent a weekly stream of free ebooks, again from my publishing company Valerian Press. You can expect to receive at least a new, free ebook each and every week. Sometimes you might receive a massive 10 free books in a week!

All you need to do is simply click here

Alternatively you can type this link into your browser: http://bit.ly/18hmup4

About The Author

Hi, I'm Martin Rowland! Thanks for visiting my page, if you have read any of my books I sincerely hope they brought a lot of value into your life. If you haven't, what are you waiting for! A life full of health, energy and abundance await you, should you apply that you learn from my books. Clean Eating is my absolute passion, ever since I took the plunge a few years back my life has been phenomenal. I have competed in marathons, seen my abs for the very first time and completely transformed my mental health. When I meet people who haven't seen me since my transformation they are stunned. It's all down to clean eating.

Outside of writing and passionately preaching about clean diets I like to spend my time reading great fiction. I can often be found spending entire weekends sitting next to the lake beside my house engrossed in a novel. It has taken me a long time to get around to it, but I am finally enjoying the wonderful work that is George Martins' A Song of Ice and Fire series. Isn't it just brilliant? My other favourite thing to do is sailing. On the weekends where you can't find me beside the lake I will be cruising along the south coast on my wonderful yacht 'Poppy'.

Please get involved with my social media accounts, I try to keep the content inspiring or thought provoking.

Facebook - https://www.facebook.com/CleanFoodDiet

Valerian Press

At Valerian Press we have three key beliefs.

Providing outstanding value: We believe in enriching all of our customers' lives, doing everything we can to ensure the best experience.

Championing new talent: We believe in showcasing the worlds emerging talent by giving them the platform to grow.

Simplicity and efficiency: We understand how valuable your time is. Our products are stream-lined and consist only of what you want. You will find no fluff with us.

We hope you have enjoyed reading Jessica's guide to the vegan diet.

We would love to offer you a regular supply of our free and discounted books. We cover a huge range of non-fiction genres; diet and cookbooks, health and fitness, alternative and holistic medicine, spirituality and plenty more. All you need to do is simply click here! Alternatively you can type this link into your web browser: http://bit.ly/18hmup4

Made in the USA
Middletown, DE
02 November 2015